CREATIVE
NATURAL
COOKBOOK

Priscilla Gove Heininger

Ruth Knighton Malinowski

Bonanza Books
New York

About the Authors

Priscilla Gove Heininger, a native Vermonter, is married and has three children. She is a home economist with a wide range of experience in nutrition, home gardening, and natural foods.

Ruth Knighton Malinowski teaches food and nutrition at the University of Maryland and is a nutrition consultant for the school lunch program. She has authored several cookbooks.

Acknowledgment

We wish to thank our husbands and families for their helpful suggestions and endless patience in tasting these recipes.

1985 edition published by Bonanza Books,
distributed by Crown Publishers, Inc.
Copyright © 1985, 1979 by Ottenheimer Publishers, Inc.
All rights reserved.
ISBN: 0-517-60583-X
Published under arrangement with Ottenheimer Publishers, Inc.
Printed in Brazil
h g f e d c b a

contents

introduction

Recently the term "natural foods" has appeared everywhere. To the consumer this term often means confusion. What is "natural"? Is anything natural anymore?

Some people define natural foods as foods grown only organically, without the use of chemical fertilizers. To others natural is the basic food containing no additives or preservatives; that is, in its natural state, but without specific references as to the method by which it is grown. We feel that preferences in origin of foods depend on an individual's values.

Since the term "natural" may include everything from prepared mixes with no chemical additives to foods grown and preserved in a home garden, our definition will draw from both sides, with emphasis on "back to the basics," or the methods of cooking "from scratch" that our grandmothers used. Our goal is to present a variety of delicious, nutritious additive-free recipes that can be prepared from basic, easily found ingredients. Sometimes these basic ingredients may include the conveniences of canned or frozen foods, because today's cook may not always find it possible to grow and preserve the entire food supply. However, basic may include the choice of mixing and baking your own graham crackers from scratch. By including a wide variety of recipes, this book will provide the chance to try both practical and fun recipes using basic ingredients.

basic ingredients

Basic ingredients in natural-foods cooking include as many unprocessed foods as possible. Whole grains, unrefined flours, beans, nuts, and seeds play an important role. Emphasis is on using fewer highly refined ingredients, such as white sugar, and placing the focus on the "straight from nature" alternative, such as honey. The use of sugar, also, is kept to a minimum with preference on fresh or dried fruits as the dietary source of this.

Many ingredients for cooking naturally may be found in local supermarkets. Some, however, are not and must be purchased at specialty food stores or through food cooperatives. As you acquire a taste for certain foods and learn to incorporate them into your daily eating patterns, joining a local food co-op, if one exists in your area, can be very beneficial.

If natural cooking is a new experience for you, begin gradually. The taste of whole grains, or the "real" flavor instead of an artificial one, will be noticeable in your meals. Children, especially, should be introduced to whole grains and unfamiliar foods over a period of time. Start by adding small proportions of whole grains to what you now cook, then wait until the flavor becomes familiar before adding more. Be patient! To help develop this taste, we have included recipes with both unbleached and whole-grain flours.

The principles for serving nutritious meals are the same in using natural foods as in any type of cooking. The "Basic Four" food groups, as developed by the United States Department of Agriculture, provide a guide in planning nutritious meals. For adults these include two servings of milk or milk products; four servings of fruits and vegetables; two or more servings of meat, poultry, fish, or eggs; and four or more servings of enriched or whole-grain breads and cereals each day. Included in the fruit and vegetable group is one serving of citrus fruit or other good source of ascorbic acid (vitamin C) each day and one serving of a dark green, yellow, or orange vegetable every other day as a source of vitamin A. Since the Basic Four food groups cover practically every food available, it is important to vary one's choice of foods each day within each group. The greater the variety of foods eaten within a diet, the more chance there is of providing adequate amounts of trace elements. The body is a delicate balance of chemical interactions that depend on the presence of many different food elements at one time in order to work together. Including as much variety as possible in food selections and using the Basic Four as a guideline for these choices assures allowing the necessary nutrients to work together in providing good health.

As you explore the world of eating naturally, you will become aware of the variety of foods available and choices that we cannot begin to cover in one book. As you experience new recipes and acquire tastes for whole grains and "old-fashioned" cooking, we hope that you and your family will become "spoiled," knowing how good foods can really taste. Package mixes may have their merits, but they can never replace basic "from-scratch" cooking! In turning to natural foods and nutritious additive-free recipes that are prepared from basic ingredients, you are better able to know exactly what you are eating because you have put those ingredients there yourself. We hope you will enjoy the opportunity to try some of our favorite natural-food recipes.

special ingredients

Here is a brief explanation of some of the ingredients used in the recipes in this book and natural-foods cooking in general:

unbleached flour

Although unbleached or all-purpose flour is not as popular as whole-grain flours in natural-foods cookery, we have included it in some recipes. There are times when taste, texture, or finished product merit its use. In choosing all-purpose or unbleached flour, always use enriched flour to which some of the key nutrients have been returned. Unbleached flour has the advantage of being less refined than bleached white all-purpose flour and is high in the necessary gluten for breadmaking.

whole-wheat pastry flour

This whole-wheat flour is a boon to the homemaker who loves to bake. It is ground from soft wheat and is lower than regular whole-wheat flour in gluten. As its name implies, it is excellent for baking pastries, quick breads, cakes, and cookies, because it gives the product a tender, flaky crust. It can replace unbleached or all-purpose white flour cup for cup in most recipes, with similar product results. Whole-wheat pastry flour can be used in all baked goods except yeast breads, which depend on a higher gluten content for their structure. It can be purchased at specialty stores or most food co-ops. Many of our baked-goods recipes call for whole-wheat pastry flour. If it is not available, substitute all-purpose flour, cup for cup. Whole-wheat flour also can be used; this substitution is described below.

whole-wheat flour

Thought of as the "staff of life," whole-wheat flour is the flour "Gramma" used. It is ground from hard winter wheat and can be used in all baked goods. The resulting product will be heavier than that made with unbleached flour. If you do not use whole-wheat flour regularly, change your baking habits to it step by step as you discover your own likes and dislikes. If whole-wheat flour is sifted, it may be substituted cup for cup for whole-wheat pastry flour; otherwise use only 7/8 cup of whole-wheat flour for each cup of pastry or all-purpose flour. To prevent rancidity, both whole-wheat pastry flour and whole-wheat flour should be stored in a cool place, such as a refrigerator or freezer.

triticale flour

Triticale is a new grain that was originally a cross between wheat and rye. Triticale flour contains a high protein content but is low in gluten, so it must be used in combination with other flours in baking, much the same as rye flour. It has a sweet, nutty flavor and, when used in correct proportions with other flours, produces a nutritious, tasty product.

other specialty flours

These flours include rye, buckwheat, oat, rice, soybean, and cornmeal. Each produces its own characteristic flavor when added to baked products. This type of flour is usually combined with unbleached or whole-wheat flour because, alone, the resulting product would be heavy and unacceptable by modern baking standards.

whole grains

Soaked and cooked until tender, whole grains are then eaten as cereals or added to other dishes. Some, such as brown rice and barley, make delicious casserole extenders as well as complementing other foods. Also, whole grains may be sprouted or purchased as flakes, such as rolled oats and wheat flakes, and added to baked goods. In flake form they make delicious granola-type cereals. Whole grains are also ground and used as flour. All forms of whole grains should be stored at a cool temperature.

dried peas and beans

These protein extenders come in a seemingly endless variety. There are black, red, white, mung, navy, soldier, yellow-eye, lima, soy, aduki, and other beans. Your familiarity will probably be reflected by the tastes and popularity of those available in your region. Likewise, members of the pea family are available in various kinds, such as whole dried peas, split peas (yellow and green), garbanzos, and lentils.

Legumes, when combined with other sources of protein, work together to provide complete protein. Cooked, they are used in soups, salads, and casseroles. Uncooked, they may be sprouted and served in salads, sandwiches, or main dishes.

Generally, to cook dried peas or beans, wash, then soak them overnight in twice as much water as beans. In the morning bring the same water and beans to a boil, then lower the heat and simmer until tender. A shorter method for tenderizing beans is to cover beans with cold water, bring them to a boil, and simmer them for 5 minutes. Remove the beans from heat, cover tightly, and let them stand for 1 hour. This takes the place of soaking beans overnight. Proceed to cook beans until tender, according to package or recipe directions. The amount of cooking time required varies with each type of bean. Most beans double in volume with soaking and cooking, although some, such as soybeans, will expand three times.

sprouts

Popular types of sprouting seeds include alfalfa, clover, mung bean, fenugreek, radish, chia, sesame, flax, and lentil. Try sprouting grains, such as wheat or rye, or other vegetable and herb seeds for variety. The list is practically endless! Choose only seeds that are labeled especially for sprouting. They may be purchased at specialty food stores. *Do not sprout seeds purchased for gardening or sold to be grown,* as many have been treated with pesticides or dyes and can be harmful if eaten. Check with your state extension service if you have questions about types to try or origins of the seeds.

When sprouting seeds, darkness and a room temperature of 65 to 70°F are best. Warmer temperatures promote mold growth. See "Starting Sprouts" (see Index) for a specific method.

When are the sprouts ready to eat? Smaller seeds, such as alfalfa, may be grown up to 1 inch long, but some larger varieties are best when only ¼ to ½ inch long. Taste and experiment to know what you prefer.

Imagination is the key to using sprouts. Eaten alone as snacks, they are nutritious and delicious. Sprouts, especially alfalfa sprouts, substitute for lettuce in sandwiches and have the same advantage of staying crisp and crunchy. For this same reason, sprouts are excellent salad additions. Try adding them to soups, vegetables, and breads. Be creative and enjoy sprouts!

nuts and seeds

Nuts and seeds are added to foods for their nutritional value, flavor, and texture. Nuts are served as snacks or ground into nut butters. In natural-foods cooking, both nuts and seeds are welcome additions to cookies, vegetables, salads, and granolas, since they are an added source of protein, vitamins, and minerals. Because of the high fat content, shelled nuts should be refrigerated or frozen to prolong freshness. Seeds may be kept in a cool, dry place.

fruits and vegetables

Natural-foods cookery takes advantage of the important nutrients that fresh fruits and vegetables contribute to the diet. The key to using vegetables lies in freshness and in eating them either raw or crisp-cooked, in order to preserve as many vitamins as possible.

Fruits, naturally sweet, contribute a healthy replacement for candy. They make good snacks and desserts as well as adding color and flavor to main dishes. Many kinds of dried fruits are available and play an important role in natural dishes. Also, these serve as nutritious snacks by themselves or in combination with nuts and seeds.

oils and butter

Much has been written about kinds of fats. Although fats in the American diet have gained a bad reputation, a certain amount is necessary for both energy and utilization of fat-soluble vitamins. The controversy lies in the types of fats eaten—animal versus vegetable, saturated versus unsaturated, and liquid versus solid.

Our main concern relative to natural foods is in simplicity. Therefore, butter is specified in most recipes because it is less refined and contains the least number of additives. If you have a problem with cholesterol, substitute a lightly polyunsaturated margarine for butter. In recipes calling for vegetable oil, we recommend safflower oil because it is the most polyunsaturated oil. Preferences and availability will determine your choice of oils.

Unrefined or cold-pressed oils are perferred in natural cooking by some persons because they have been subjected to less processing. Refrigerate unprocessed oils to prevent rancidity.

sweeteners

Preference is given to honey, maple syrup, molasses, and brown sugar as sweeteners because they contain trace elements, as opposed to refined (cane) sugar which supplies only "empty calories."

It is generally recognized that all sugars play too large a role in the American diet and should be limited. As a person begins to cut down sugar intake, "taste" for sweets decreases. (The process is also reversible!) Although fruits, both dried and fresh, provide a natural sweet touch at the end of a meal, there are times when we all love other types of sweet desserts. For this reason, cookies, cakes, and other desserts are included in this book with the hope that they will be eaten wisely and will not replace other nutritious foods in meals. In these desserts sugar has been kept to a minimum and other nutritious ingredients have been included so that they will provide some good nutrition at the same time.

yeast

The yeast in these recipes is measured both by specific amount, such as 1 tablespoon, and by the number of packages. The reasons for this are that active dry yeast obtained at the grocery store in individual packets contains a preservative and is expensive, particularly if you bake a lot. By contrast, active dry yeast granules, which can be purchased by the pound (or part of a pound) at specialty food stores, have no added preservatives and cost less per ounce. A scant tablespoon of these active dry yeast granules is equal to one ¼-ounce package of dry yeast. Active dry yeast granules can be dissolved in warm water and used the same as any dry yeast, except where the yeast is first combined with flour. In those recipes, whirl dry granules in a blender before combining them with flour, to assure a more uniform distribution.

Dry-yeast granules should be stored in an airtight container in a cool, dry atmosphere for up to six months, or frozen for longer storage. For the busy cook, a jar of yeast granules stored in a freezer door within easy reach is particularly handy. The frozen yeast granules can be measured out when needed and, if not used regularly, will still remain active.

appetizers

stuffed pepper slices

stuffed pepper slices

Yield: 4 to 6 servings

    1 red pepper
    1 green pepper
    8 ounces cottage cheese
    2 tablespoons milk
    1 tablespoon chopped pimiento
    1 tablespoon chopped parsley
    1 tablespoon chopped watercress
    1 tablespoon chopped chives
    $1/4$ teaspoon salt
    $1/8$ teaspoon white pepper
    1 teaspoon lemon juice
    1 envelope (1 tablespoon) unflavored gelatin
    $1/3$ cup cold water
    Lettuce leaves

Cut tops off peppers. Remove seeds; wash.

Cream cottage cheese in blender (thin with milk if necessary); remove. Add pimiento, parsley, watercress, chives, salt, pepper, and lemon juice.

Soak gelatin in cold water; dissolve completely over simmering water. Add to cheese mixture. Fill peppers with mixture; chill in refrigerator at least 2 hours.

Cut each pepper into 4 thick slices. Serve on lettuce.

soft cheese spread

A cooking thermometer and cheesecloth are essential for preparing this recipe.

Yield: 1 cup

2 quarts skim milk
2 cups buttermilk
1 teaspoon salt
1 teaspoon black pepper
1 tablespoon coarsely ground black pepper

In large saucepan heat skim milk and buttermilk to 170°F. Stir occasionally to prevent scorching. Maintain temperature between 170 and 175°F until curds form in milk, about 30 minutes or more.

Meanwhile dampen 1 yard cheesecloth; fold in thirds. Line colander with cheesecloth. Using slotted spoon, place curds in colander to drain. Discard remaining liquid (the whey). Drain curds about 1 hour.

Mash curds to remove additional water. Scrape cheese from cheesecloth into bowl. Mix in salt and regular pepper. Form 2 or more balls or other shapes with cheese; sprinkle surfaces with coarse black pepper.

Serve spread with crackers or toast.

brie crackers

Yield: About 5 dozen

½ cup butter or margarine, softened
8 ounces Brie cheese, room temperature
½ cup all-purpose flour
½ cup whole-wheat flour
1/8 teaspoon cayenne pepper
¼ teaspoon salt
½ cup sesame seeds

Beat all ingredients except sesame seeds in medium-size bowl. Divide mixture in half; form each half into long round roll. Wrap waxed paper around each roll; refrigerate at least 12 hours.

Slice chilled rolls into ¼-inch rounds. Sprinkle with sesame seeds. Place on cookie sheets. Bake at 400°F 12 minutes. Cool; store in tightly covered container.

swiss-cheese squares

swiss-cheese squares

Yield: 1½ dozen

    2 cups all-purpose flour
    2½ teaspoons baking powder
    ½ teaspoon baking soda
    1 teaspoon salt
    ⅓ cup shortening
    ½ cup buttermilk
    1 cup grated Swiss cheese (4 ounces)
    1 egg, beaten
    2 tablespoons poppy seeds

Sift flour, baking powder, baking soda, and salt. Cut in shortening with pastry blender or 2 knives until mixture resembles dry cornmeal. Add enough milk to form soft dough that cleans side of bowl. Knead cheese into dough 1 to 2 minutes. Roll dough to ½ inch thick. Cut into squares, using scalloped knife or pizza cutter. Brush tops with egg; sprinkle with poppy seeds. Place on ungreased cookie sheet. Bake in preheated 450°F oven 10 minutes or until golden brown. Best when served hot.

seafood cocktail

Yield: 4 servings

> 1 orange
> 16 blue grapes, some halved and seeded
> Bibb lettuce leaves
> 1 8-ounce can white or green asparagus tips
> 12 ounces canned or cooked seafood (crab, shrimp, lobster, etc.,
>   thoroughly chilled)
> Cooked crab claws for garnish
> Unpeeled orange slices for garnish

cocktail dressing

> ¼ cup mayonnaise
> ¼ cup plain yogurt
> 1 teaspoon catsup
> 1 teaspoon prepared horseradish
> 2 teaspoons lemon juice
> Salt and pepper to taste

Cut peel from orange; remove white membrane. Slice orange; cut each slice into quarters.

Line cocktail glasses with lettuce. Arrange orange pieces, grape halves, and asparagus on lettuce. Place seafood on top.

Blend together all dressing ingredients. Pour about 2 tablespoons dressing over top of each cocktail. Garnish each with half slice of orange, whole grapes, and crab claw. Serve at once.

seafood cocktail

soups

asparagus soup

Yield: 6 servings

> **30 stalks asparagus (about 2 pounds)**
> **4 quarts water**
> **1 tablespoon salt**
> **¼ cup minced onion**
> **¼ cup minced parsley**
> **1 teaspoon ground coriander**
> **2 tablespoons butter or margarine**
> **1 tablespoon flour**
> **2 cups chicken broth, heated**
> **½ cup light (table) cream**
> **1 tablespoon lemon juice**
> **½ teaspoon salt**
> **¼ teaspoon white pepper**

Peel asparagus with potato peeler; trim tough ends. Tie together in 3 bunches; simmer in large pot of salted water until just tender. Lift out bundles; place in sink of cold water. When cool, drain on paper towels. Cut tips from stalks; reserve. Cut stalks into 1-inch pieces; reserve.

Sauté onion and parsley with coriander and butter in medium saucepan until vegetables are softened. Stir in flour; cook 3 minutes. Remove pan from heat. Stir in broth; simmer 5 minutes. Add asparagus stalks.

Puree mixture in blender or food mill until smooth. Do this by batches. Return puree to saucepan; stir in cream and asparagus tips; heat through. Stir in lemon juice. Add salt and pepper; adjust seasonings to taste. Serve soup hot or chilled.

cheese–vegetable soup

Yield: 6 servings

½ cup chopped carrot
½ cup chopped onion
½ cup chopped celery
2 cups chicken broth
2 slices bacon
1 tablespoon butter or margarine
⅓ cup flour

1½ cups milk
8 ounces sharp cheddar cheese, shredded
½ cup light (table) cream
½ teaspoon salt
⅛ teaspoon white pepper
1 sprig parsley, chopped

Add vegetables to broth in medium saucepan; simmer, covered, until tender.
Meanwhile sauté bacon in butter until crisp. Drain on paper towels; reserve.
Blend flour into remaining fat; cook 1 to 2 minutes (mixture should be thick and bubbling). Slowly blend in milk. Cook and stir until smooth and thickened. Add cheese; heat until melted.
Place hot vegetable–broth mixture in blender; puree. Add to hot cheese mixture. Stir in cream and seasonings. Heat to just below boiling.
Garnish with crumbled bacon and parsley. Serve soup hot.

gazpacho

gazpacho

Yield: 4 servings

4 medium tomatoes, peeled, chopped
1 small onion, chopped
1 green pepper, seeded, chopped
⅛ teaspoon garlic powder
2 tablespoons lemon juice
½ teaspoon salt
Dash of freshly ground pepper
Sliced cucumbers
Chopped onions
Croutons

Puree tomatoes, onion, and green pepper in blender. Add garlic powder, lemon juice, salt, and pepper.
Serve gazpacho chilled with garnishes of cucumber slices, chopped onions, and croutons, or serve side dishes of finely chopped tomatoes, onions, and green pepper.

beef vegetable soup

Yield: 6 main-course servings

1½ pounds boneless round steak,
    cut into ½-inch cubes
3 tablespoons vegetable oil
1 medium onion, chopped
2 carrots, chopped
½ green pepper, chopped
2 stalks celery, chopped

1½ cups chopped cabbage
2 tablespoons tomato paste
1 teaspoon salt
½ teaspoon pepper
1 parsley stalk
1 bay leaf
½ teaspoon thyme

Brown meat in hot oil in Dutch oven. Remove; reserve.

Add vegetables (except tomato paste) to Dutch oven; stir-cook until wilted. Return meat to Dutch oven. Add remaining ingredients. Pour in enough boiling water to cover ingredients. Cover; simmer gently about 2 hours or until meat is tender. Remove bay leaf and parsley.

Serve soup with French bread for a light and nutritious dinner.

beef vegetable soup

vichyssoise

Yield: 4 servings

3 to 4 leeks or green onions
2 tablespoons butter or margarine
1 medium onion, chopped
2 large potatoes, peeled, diced
½ teaspoon salt
3 cups chicken broth

1½ cups milk
1 cup heavy cream
1 drop Tabasco sauce
1 tablespoon minced parsley or chives

Thoroughly clean leeks. Halve lengthwise; cut into thin slices.

Heat butter. Add leeks and onion; cook until transparent. Add potatoes, salt, and broth; simmer 35 minutes. Puree in blender or food mill; reheat. Pour in milk and ½ cup cream. Heat and stir until well blended, but do not boil. Season with Tabasco sauce. Chill mixture.

Beat ½ cup cream until stiff; fold into soup. Adjust seasonings.

Serve soup garnished with chopped chives or parsley.

broccoli chowder

Yield: 4 servings

1 pound fresh broccoli
1½ cups chicken broth
1½ cups milk
½ cup chopped cooked ham
¼ teaspoon freshly ground pepper
1½ cups grated Swiss cheese (6 ounces)
2 tablespoons butter or margarine
Salt to taste

broccoli chowder

Wash broccoli; remove leaves and coarse stem ends.

Pour broth into large pot; bring to boil. Add broccoli. Reduce heat; simmer, uncovered, 3 minutes. Cover; cook 10 minutes or until broccoli is just tender. Remove broccoli with slotted spoon; chop into bite-size pieces.

Add milk, ham, and pepper to stock. Bring to boil, stirring occasionally. Stir in cheese, butter, and broccoli; heat until cheese is melted. Add salt to taste. Do not boil. Serve hot.

meat

stuffed flank steak

Yield: 4 to 6 servings

2 pounds flank steak, scored, or 2 round steaks, thinly sliced
2 tablespoons Dijon-style mustard
¼ teaspoon thyme

Spread meat with mustard; sprinkle with thyme.

spinach stuffing

½ package frozen spinach, cooked, drained
½ cup chopped onions
1 tablespoon bacon fat or vegetable oil
½ cup raw sausage meat
1 egg
½ teaspoon salt
⅛ teaspoon allspice
⅛ teaspoon pepper
1 clove garlic, crushed
¼ cup dry bread crumbs

Squeeze all water from spinach.

Sauté onions in fat. Add spinach; toss. Add sausage, egg, salt, allspice, pepper, garlic, and crumbs to spinach mixture; mix well. Spread stuffing on meat; roll up jelly-roll fashion. Tie with string.

6 slices bacon
1 onion, chopped
1 carrot, chopped
½ cup dry white wine
1 can beef broth

Cook bacon in Dutch oven until partly done; remove.

Add meat to Dutch oven; brown on all sides (about 10 minutes). Lay bacon over meat. Add onion, carrot, wine, and broth; bring to simmer. Place in 325°F oven about 1 hour or until tender.

Place meat on platter. Strain juices, pressing hard on vegetables. If desired, thicken with 1 tablespoon cornstarch dissolved in water.

Slice meat; serve with pan juices.

beef goulash

beef goulash

Yield: 4 servings

    1 pound lean beef (round steak)
    2 tablespoons vegetable oil
    1 large onion, chopped
    1 pound potatoes, peeled, cubed
    1 green pepper, cut into strips
    2 tomatoes, peeled, cut into chunks
    1 clove garlic, minced
    ½ teaspoon caraway seeds
    1 3-inch piece lemon peel, minced
    2 teaspoons paprika
    ½ teaspoon salt
    2 cups beef bouillon

Pat meat dry with paper towels. Cut into strips approximately ½ inch wide and 2 inches long.

Heat oil in 4-quart Dutch oven. Add meat and onion; cook 5 minutes or until brown. Add potatoes; cook 5 minutes. Add remaining ingredients. Cover; simmer over low heat 30 minutes. At end of cooking time, uncover; boil liquid a few minutes, until reduced. Correct seasoning if necessary.

scandinavian pot roast

Yield: 6 servings

¼ cup vegetable oil
1 3-pound rump or round roast
¼ pound small fresh mushrooms
3 medium onions, thinly sliced
1 clove garlic
½ teaspoon salt
¼ teaspoon pepper

¼ teaspoon ginger
½ cup red wine
2 cups beef broth
12 pitted prunes
¼ cup black olives, drained
Parsley for garnish

Heat oil in large Dutch oven; brown meat on all sides. Remove meat; reserve. Sauté mushrooms in same oil. Remove; reserve.

Add onions and garlic to oil; cook until onions are soft and golden. Drain off remaining oil. Return meat to Dutch oven. Add seasonings, wine, and broth. Cook, covered, in 300°F oven 2 hours. Add prunes and olives; cook 1 hour or until roast is tender. Add mushrooms; heat through.

Place roast on platter; surround with mushrooms, prunes, and olives. If desired, reduce stock by boiling. Pour over meat, or serve separately. Sprinkle top of roast and sauce with finely chopped parsley.

scandinavian pot roast

ham and fruit in pineapple

Yield: 2 servings

1 fresh pineapple

ham stuffing

6 ounces cooked ham, cubed
6 ounces sauerkraut
1 medium apple

salad dressing

3 tablespoons mayonnaise
2 tablespoons light (table) cream
Juice of 1 lemon
1 teaspoon fresh chopped dill or ¼ teaspoon dried dill
¼ teaspoon rosemary
¼ teaspoon sugar
Salt if desired

Cut pineapple into half lengthwise; scoop out. Cut into bite-size pieces.
Cube ham.
Rinse and drain sauerkraut.
Core unpeeled apple; cut into thin slices.
Gently mix above ingredients. Fill pineapple halves with Ham Stuffing.
Thoroughly blend mayonnaise, cream, lemon juice, dill, rosemary, sugar, and salt. Pour dressing over salad. Let marinate and chill in refrigerator 30 minutes.

braised veal rolls

braised veal rolls

Yield: 4 servings

    4 veal scallops or cutlets
    1 onion, chopped
    4 tablespoons vegetable oil
    4 ounces mushrooms, minced
        (about 1 cup)
    1 clove garlic, minced
    2 large carrots, chopped
    1 large onion, chopped
    ¾ cup white wine
    ¾ cup beef broth
    ½ teaspoon salt
    ⅛ teaspoon pepper
    ¼ teaspoon thyme
    1 bay leaf
    1 tablespoon butter or margarine
    1 tablespoon flour
    Parlsey for garnish

Pound veal to tenderize and flatten.

In large frypan sauté 1 onion in 2 tablespoons hot oil until soft. Add mushrooms; cook 5 minutes. Spread onion–mushroom mixture on each slice of meat. Roll up; tie with string.

Brown veal in 2 tablespoons hot oil. Remove; reserve. Drain excess oil.

Add garlic, carrots, large onion, wine, broth, salt, pepper, thyme, and bay leaf to frypan. Heat to simmer. Add veal; cover. Simmer 1½ hours.

When veal is done, remove strings from rolls. Place on serving dish; keep warm.

Remove bay leaf from sauce. Pour sauce into electric blender; puree.

If thicker sauce is desired, melt butter in saucepan. Stir in flour; make smooth paste. Add sauce, stirring constantly; heat to boiling point. Reduce heat to simmer; cook 1 to 2 minutes, until sauce thickens.

Pour sauce over veal rolls; garnish with chopped parsley. Serve with boiled potatoes if desired.

party pork chops

fresh vegetables with pork

Yield: 8 servings

> 8 thick-sliced (¾-inch) pork chops
> 8 onion slices, about ¼ inch thick
> 8 fresh lemon slices, about ¼ inch thick, from midsections of 2 unpeeled lemons
> ⅔ cup brown sugar
> 1¼ teaspoons salt
> ¼ teaspoon pepper
> 3 tablespoons fresh lemon juice
> ⅔ cup chili sauce

Place pork in single layer in baking pan. Place 1 onion slice topped with 1 lemon slice on center of each chop.

Blend remaining ingredients; spoon over each chop. Cover pan tightly. Bake in 350°F oven 1½ hours or until pork is tender.

fresh vegetables with pork

Yield: 6 servings

> 2 tablespoons vegetable oil
> 6 stalks celery, sliced diagonally
> ½ pound mushrooms, halved
> 1 medium green pepper, sliced
> 1 medium red pepper, sliced
> 1 medium onion, sliced
> 1 pound boneless pork, cut into ½-inch cubes
> 1 cup chicken broth
> 1 tablespoon soy sauce
> 1 tablespoon cornstarch
> ½ teaspoon ginger
> ¼ teaspoon pepper

Heat oil in wok or frypan. Stir-fry celery about 4 minutes. Add mushrooms, peppers, and onion; stir-fry 5 minutes. Remove vegetables; reserve.

Add pork to pan; stir-fry 5 minutes. Add broth; stir in vegetables. Simmer 5 minutes.

Meanwhile blend soy sauce with cornstarch, ginger, and pepper. Stir into pork and vegetable mixture; cook, stirring constantly, about 3 minutes or until heated and thickened.

Serve mixture over rice.

corned beef–stuffed potatoes

Yield: 4 servings

4 large baking potatoes
1½ cups minced cooked corned beef
¼ cup butter or margarine
Salt and pepper to taste
⅛ cup minced fresh parsley
4 eggs

Bake potatoes at 400°F 1 hour or until done. Cut slice off top of each potato; scoop out centers. Leave ¼ to ½ inch potato around walls. Mash potatoes. Stir in corned beef and butter. Add salt and pepper. Divide mixture among potatoes; reheat.

Meanwhile poach eggs.

Sprinkle tops of potatoes with parsley; top with cooked eggs. Serve as a main dish.

corned-beef stuffed potatoes

sausage pizza

sausage pizza

Yield: 12-inch pizza

pizza crust

> 1 package active dry
>   yeast
> ½ cup warm water
>   (105 to 115°F)
> ¾ cup all-purpose flour
>   and ¾ cup whole wheat flour
>   (or 1½ cups all-purpose flour
>   if desired)
> ½ teaspoon salt
> 1 teaspoon sugar
> 1 tablespoon vegetable oil

pizza sauce

> ¼ cup chopped onion
> 1 tablespoon vegetable oil
> 1 16-ounce can tomatoes
> 3 tablespoons tomato paste
> 1 teaspoon oregano
> ½ teaspoon salt
> 1/8 teaspoon freshly ground black pepper

pizza toppings*

> 1 tablespoon vegetable oil
> ¼ to ½ pound bulk sausage
> 6 ounces mozzarella cheese, shredded
> 2 tablespoons Parmesan cheese

> *Other toppings, such as mushrooms, ham, anchovy fillets, pepperoni, etc.,
>   can be added if desired.

In medium bowl dissolve yeast in warm water.

Combine flours, salt, and sugar in separate bowl. Add flour mixture and oil to yeast; stir well. Turn out onto floured board; knead until smooth and elastic, about 6 to 8 minutes.

Lightly grease bowl. Place dough in bowl; turn once to grease top surface. Cover; let rise until double in bulk (about 1½ hours).

Meanwhile in medium frypan sauté onion in hot oil until tender. Add remaining sauce ingredients. Break up tomato pieces with fork. Bring sauce to boil; reduce heat to low. Cook, partially covered, 50 minutes or until thick; cool.

When dough has doubled in bulk, punch down. Roll out into 12-inch circle; place on round pizza pan or cookie sheet. Brush lightly with oil. Let rise 10 minutes. Bake crust 10 minutes in preheated 400°F oven.

While crust is cooking, lightly fry sausage. Remove the crust from oven; top with sauce. Then top with sausage; sprinkle cheeses over all. Bake 12 minutes or until cheese is melted and lightly browned. Remove pizza from pan; cut and enjoy.

vegetable stew with lamb

Yield: 6 servings

2 tablespoons vegetable oil
1 pound lean lamb, cut into bite-size pieces
1 medium onion, chopped
1 small head cabbage, shredded
1 stalk celery, sliced
2 medium carrots, sliced
1 stalk leek, sliced
6 cups hot beef bouillon
2 medium potatoes, cubed
1 small head cauliflower, separated into florets
1 10-ounce package frozen green beans
2 tablespoons tomato paste
½ teaspoon salt
¼ teaspoon white pepper
Parsley to garnish

Heat oil in 4-quart Dutch oven or saucepan. Brown meat about 5 minutes. Add onion; sauté until golden brown. Add cabbage, celery, carrots, leek, and bouillon. Bring to boil; simmer 1 hour. Add potatoes, cauliflower, and beans. Simmer 20 to 30 minutes, until vegetables are tender.

Thin tomato paste with a little broth; add to stew. Season with salt and pepper. Garnish stew with chopped parsley.

vegetable stew with lamb

poultry

chicken lentil casserole

Yield: 4 to 5 servings

  1 cup lentils
  2½ cups water
  3 tablespoons butter or margarine
  ½ pound mushrooms, sliced
  1 medium onion, chopped
  1 large carrot, chopped
  1 medium potato, chopped
  1 tablespoon all-purpose flour
  1½ cups seasoned chicken broth
  ¾ teaspoon salt
  ⅛ teaspoon pepper
  ¾ teaspoon dillweed
  1 cup chopped cooked chicken
  1 cup buttered whole-wheat bread crumbs

Wash lentils. Place in saucepan; cover with water. Bring to boil; cover. Simmer over low heat 20 minutes.

Melt 2 tablespoons butter in frying pan. Sauté mushrooms lightly. Remove mushrooms; set aside.

Add remaining butter to pan. Sauté onion, carrot, and potato until onion is soft. Stir in flour; mix thoroughly. Add broth, salt, pepper, and dillweed; boil, stirring, about 1 minute. Remove from heat. Add mushrooms and chicken.

Drain lentils. Stir into sauce. Pour into 1½-quart casserole dish. Top with buttered bread crumbs. Bake at 350°F about 30 minutes, until lightly browned and bubbly.

chicken paprika

Yield: 4 servings

1 chicken, 2½ to 3 pounds
1 tablespoon vegetable oil
1 large onion, chopped
2 tablespoons paprika
1 clove garlic, minced
½ teaspoon salt
1 teaspoon caraway seeds
1 cup hot water
1 scallion or leek, cut lengthwise, sliced

1 small carrot, sliced
1 small stalk celery, sliced
2 medium potatoes, peeled, cubed
½ cup chicken broth or bouillon
3 tomatoes
1 red pepper, cubed
1 green pepper, cubed
Parsley for garnish

Skin and bone chicken; cut into bite-size pieces.

Heat oil in 4-quart Dutch oven; sauté onion. Sprinkle 1 tablespoon paprika over onion; stir well. Add garlic, salt, caraway seeds, and ½ cup hot water. Simmer over low heat 10 minutes. Add chicken pieces; cover. Simmer 5 minutes. Add ½ cup water; cover. Simmer 15 minutes. Add scallion, carrot, celery, potatoes, and broth. Simmer 10 minutes.

Peel and chop 2 tomatoes.

Add peppers, chopped tomatoes, and 1 tablespoon paprika to chicken; cover. Simmer 15 minutes. Correct seasoning if necessary.

Serve chicken garnished with 1 sliced tomato and chopped parsley.

chicken paprika

tomatoes stuffed with chicken

Yield: 6 servings

½ teaspoon salt
¼ teaspoon tarragon
1 cup plain yogurt
1 can (8 ounces) crushed pineapple, drained
1½ cups diced cooked chicken
½ cup toasted slivered almonds
1 stalk celery, finely diced
6 tomatoes

To prepare dressing, stir salt and tarragon into yogurt; chill.
In separate bowl combine pineapple, chicken, almonds, and celery; chill.
Just before serving, stir dressing lightly into chicken mixture.
Cut tomatoes partially into sections; fill with salad. Garnish with parsley, if desired.

egg foo yung

Yield: 4 servings

1 small onion
1 tomato
½ cup cooked chicken
¼ cup canned sliced water chestnuts
3 scallions, thinly sliced
2 tablespoons soy sauce
3 large mushrooms, sliced

2 eggs, slightly beaten
2 tablespoons vegetable oil
1 cup sprouts (see Index, or buy bean sprouts)
2 teaspoons sugar
1½ teaspoons cornstarch
¾ cup water

Peel onion. Cut in half lengthwise; cut halves into ½-inch-wide lengthwise strips.

Cut tomato in half and into thin lengthwise wedges.

Place chicken in bowl. Add water chestnuts, scallions, 1 tablespoon soy sauce, mushrooms, and eggs; mix together lightly.

Heat 1 tablespoon oil in small heavy frypan. Spoon about ¼ of egg mixture into frypan. Spread ¼ of sprouts, tomato slices, and ⅛ teaspoon sugar over egg mixture. Cook until "cake" is nicely browned on underside, about 3 minutes. Carefully turn with pancake turner; brown other side. Cook until edges are a little crisp. Remove cake; keep warm. Add more oil to frypan as necessary. Cook remaining cakes.

While cakes are cooking, mix cornstarch and 1½ teaspoons sugar in small saucepan. Add water gradually; blend until smooth. Heat to boiling. Add 1 tablespoon soy sauce; simmer 1 minute. Serve hot sauce on egg foo yung.

sweet-and-sour chicken

Yield: 4 servings

    2 tablespoons soy sauce
    1 tablespoon cornstarch
    2 whole chicken breasts, halved, skinned, boned, cut into bite-size cubes
    1 tablespoon vegetable oil
    1 cucumber, scored lengthwise with tines of fork, cut into bite-size cubes
    ½ cantaloupe, seeded, rinded, cut into bite-size pieces
    1 sweet red pepper (or green pepper), cubed

sweet-and-sour sauce

    2 tablespoons brown sugar
    2 tablespoons vinegar
    ½ cup pineapple juice (unsweetened)
    1 tablespoon cornstarch in 2 tablespoons cold water

    3 ounces blanched whole almonds

Combine soy sauce and cornstarch. Coat chicken pieces thoroughly.

Heat oil in large frypan (or wok); stir-fry chicken 3 to 4 minutes. Add cucumber, cantaloupe, and pepper.

Mix together sauce ingredients. Add to chicken mixture. Heat, stirring often, until sauce boils and ingredients are heated through. Add almonds. Serve at once.

sweet-and-sour chicken

seafood

shrimp with marinara sauce

Yield: 4 servings

> 1 quart water
> ½ teaspoon salt
> 1 bay leaf
> 1 pound large shrimp

Bring water, salt, and bay leaf to boil in saucepan. Add shrimp; boil 5 minutes. Drain; cool. Peel and devein shrimp.

marinara sauce

> 2 tablespoons vegetable oil
> 1 clove garlic, minced
> ½ small onion, chopped
> 2 cups canned pressed and drained whole or Italian tomatoes (reserve ⅓ cup juice)
> 2 finely chopped anchovy fillets
> ½ teaspoon sugar
> ½ teaspoon oregano

Heat oil in frypan; sauté garlic and onion until tender. Slowly add tomatoes; break up pieces. Stir in ⅓ cup juice, anchovies, sugar, and oregano. Bring to boil; gently simmer, uncovered, 20 minutes. Stir occasionally.
Place shrimp in lightly greased au gratin dish. Top with sauce.

topping

> 3 tablespoons dry bread crumbs
> 2 tablespoons grated Parmesan cheese
> 1 tablespoon finely chopped parsley

Combine ingredients; sprinkle over sauce. Bake in preheated 425°F oven 12 to 15 minutes.

shrimp with marinara sauce

seafood stew

Yield: 4 to 6 servings

> 2½ tablespoons butter or margarine
> 1 small onion, chopped
> 2 stalks celery, including tops, chopped
> 1 large carrot, diced
> 1 cup water
> 1 8-ounce can minced clams, including juice
> 1 8-ounce can whole shelled baby clams, including juice
> 1 pound fish fillets, cut into bite-size pieces (ocean perch, haddock, sole, etc.)
> 1 cup nonfat dry milk powder
> 1 chicken bouillon cube
> 2 large potatoes, peeled, diced
> ¼ teaspoon salt
> ⅛ teaspoon pepper
> Dash of celery salt

Melt butter in large saucepan. Sauté onion, celery, and carrot until onion is tender. Stir in water, clams, fish, milk powder, and bouillon. Add potatoes and seasonings; cover. Simmer over very low heat about 20 minutes or until potatoes are tender. Do not allow to boil.

fish fillets on spinach

Yield: 6 servings

1½ pounds fish fillets
Juice of 1 lemon
2 pounds fresh spinach
2 tablespoons vegetable oil
1 medium onion, chopped
½ teaspoon salt
⅛ teaspoon white pepper
½ teaspoon grated fresh nutmeg
2 tomatoes
¼ cup grated mozzarella cheese

Wash fish; pat dry. Sprinkle with lemon juice; let stand 10 minutes.

Wash spinach well; chop coarsely.

Heat oil in frypan. Add onion; sauté until soft. Fry fish in pan with onion few minutes on each side, until golden brown. Remove fish and onion; reserve.

Add spinach to frypan; stir-fry 4 to 5 minutes.

Grease casserole dish. Add spinach. Arrange fish fillets on top of spinach; sprinkle with salt, pepper, and nutmeg. Place sliced tomatoes on top of fish. Sprinkle with cheese. Bake in preheated 350°F oven 15 minutes.

fish fillets on spinach

bouillabaisse

Yield: 6 servings

sauce

bouillabaisse

    2 tablespoons vegetable oil
    2 onions, chopped, or 3 leeks, sliced
    4 cloves garlic, crushed
    2 fresh tomatoes, peeled, diced
    3 tablespoons tomato paste
    2 cups bottled clam juice
    4 cups chicken bouillon
    1 tablespoon salt
    $1/8$ teaspoon pepper
    ¼ teaspoon saffron
    ½ teaspoon thyme
    1 bay leaf
    6 sprigs parsley
    Grated rind of 1 orange

Heat oil in large saucepan or Dutch oven. Sauté onions several minutes, until translucent. Add remaining sauce ingredients; simmer 45 minutes.

seafoods

    1 2-pound lobster and/or other shellfish, such as clams, mussels (with shells),
       scallops, crab, or shrimp
    2 pounds assorted whitefish fillets, such as sea bass, perch, cod, sole, flounder,
       or red snapper

Chopped parsley for garnish

Prepare seafoods. Place lobster in large kettle of boiling salted water 10 minutes. Break claws and tail from body; crack claws. Cut tail into 1-inch chunks. Remove black vein from tail pieces; leave shell on meat. Wash fish fillets; cut into 2-inch pieces.

Add lobster and firm-fleshed fish (sea bass, perch, etc.) to boiling sauce; boil rapidly 5 minutes. Add tender-fleshed fish, such as clams, scallops, sole, or cod; boil 5 minutes. Lift seafoods out as soon as cooked; keep warm in soup tureen or platter.

Boil liquid 10 minutes to reduce. Strain liquid through coarse sieve into tureen, mashing through some of vegetables. Garnish with parsley.

other main dishes

puffy cheese–sprout omelet

Yield: 4 to 6 servings

> 6 eggs, separated
> ¼ cup milk
> ½ teaspoon salt
> 1½ tablespoons butter or margarine
> 1 cup alfalfa sprouts
> 1½ cups grated cheddar cheese

Beat egg yolks until thick and lemon-colored. Beat in milk and salt.

Beat egg whites until stiff but not dry. Fold yolks into whites.

Heat butter in large ovenproof frying pan. Pour in egg mixture. Spread sprouts and cheese on top of mixture, no closer than 1 inch from sides of pan. Push lightly into omelet. Cook over low heat until puffed and set and edges are golden on bottom when lifted with knife (8 to 10 minutes). Place in 325°F oven until top is brown, about 10 minutes. Garnish with fresh parsley if desired.

eggplant–cheese patties

Yield: 4 to 5 patties

> 1 medium eggplant
> 2 eggs, beaten
> 1½ cups whole-wheat bread crumbs
> 1 cup grated cheddar cheese
> 2 tablespoons grated Parmesan cheese
> 2 tablespoons wheat germ
> 2 tablespoons minced onion
> ½ teaspoon celery salt
> ¼ teaspoon dry mustard
> ¼ teaspoon salt
> ⅛ teaspoon pepper
> Dash of garlic salt

Peel eggplant; cut into 1-inch cubes. Cook, covered, in boiling, salted water 5 to 6 minutes, until tender. Drain well; chop finely. Stir in remaining ingredients. Shape into patties. Fry in butter or oil on hot griddle until golden brown on each side.

corn–cheese quiche

Yield: 6 servings

1 Single Pie Crust pastry, unbaked (see Index)
3 ears corn (or about 1 cup kernels)
4 eggs
1 cup milk
½ cup light (table) cream
½ cup freshly grated Parmesan cheese
2 tablespoons finely chopped onion
1 teaspoon salt
¼ teaspoon pepper
6 slices bacon
Parsley for garnish

Roll out pastry on floured board to ⅛ inch thick; fit into 9-inch quiche or pie pan.

Cut kernels off corncobs; reserve.

Beat eggs in large mixing bowl. Stir in milk, cream, cheese, onion, salt, and pepper; mix well. Add corn. Pour into pie shell. Bake in preheated 375°F oven 20 minutes.

Meanwhile fry bacon until almost done; drain on paper towels. Arrange bacon on top of pie; bake 10 minutes or until knife inserted in custard comes out clean.

Garnish quiche with parsley; serve hot.

corn–cheese quiche

sherman's new england baked beans

sherman's new england baked beans

Yield: 8 servings

> **1 pound dry beans**
> **(navy, pea, or soldier)**
> **6 cups cold water**
> **¼ pound salt pork,**
> **cut into ½-inch pieces**
> **1½ teaspoons salt**
> **⅓ cup brown sugar**
> **¼ cup molasses**
> **1 tablespoon vinegar**
> **¾ teaspoon dry mustard**
> **1 small onion, minced**

Rinse beans. In 3-quart saucepan or large pot add beans to cold water. Bring to boil; simmer 5 minutes. Remove from heat; cover. Let stand 1 hour. (This method saves soaking beans overnight.)

Drain beans; reserve liquid. Place beans and salt pork into 2-quart greased casserole or bean pot.

Make sauce by combining 2½ cups bean liquid and remaining ingredients. Pour liquid over beans; cover. Bake at 300°F 8 to 10 hours. Add more bean liquid or hot water when needed. Remove cover ½ hour before serving if browner beans are desired.

italian zucchini omelet

Yield: 2 servings

italian zucchini omelet

½ cup thinly sliced zucchini
2 slices onion
1 tablespoon vegetable oil
4 eggs
4 tablespoons water
¼ teaspoon basil
½ teaspoon salt
Dash of pepper
1 tablespoon butter or margarine
3 tablespoons diced fresh tomato
2 tablespoons grated Parmesan cheese

In medium ovenproof frypan sauté zucchini and onion in oil until tender. Remove vegetables with slotted spoon; reserve vegetables and oil.

Combine eggs, water, basil, salt, and pepper. Stir in cooked vegetables.

Heat butter in pan with reserved oil until hot enough to sizzle a drop of water. Pour egg mixture into hot pan. Mixture will start to set immediately. Sprinkle tomato and cheese over top of omelet. With fork, lightly pull cooked edge away from side of pan, so uncooked portions flow to bottom. When only top is uncooked, place pan 4 to 6 inches from broiler flame about 2 minutes to melt cheese and brown top. Serve at once.

brown-rice and cheese bake

Yield: 6 to 8 servings

3 cups cooked brown rice
1 tablespoon vegetable oil
½ cup chopped onion
6 ounces Swiss cheese, grated
½ cup sesame seeds
1 egg, beaten
1 cup milk
⅛ cup chopped parsley
Parsley sprigs to garnish

Sauté onion in hot oil until soft.

Combine all ingredients; place in greased casserole. Bake in preheated 350°F oven 40 minutes or until hot and slightly brown on top. Garnish with parsley sprigs.

broccoli casserole

Yield: 6 servings

> **2 pounds fresh broccoli (or 1 10-ounce package frozen broccoli)**
> **1½ cups milk**
> **3 eggs, beaten**
> **½ teaspoon salt**
> **¼ teaspoon pepper**
> **½ teaspoon nutmeg**
> **¾ cup grated cheddar cheese**

Cut fresh broccoli into spears. Peel skins off stalks; slice stalks lengthwise if thick. Steam or boil broccoli (fresh or frozen) until almost tender. Drain; reserve.

Meanwhile heat milk to lukewarm in medium saucepan. Add eggs, salt, pepper, nutmeg, and cheese. Beating constantly, heat just enough to melt cheese and blend all ingredients. Pour into greased baking dish. Add broccoli. Bake in preheated 350°F oven 30 to 40 minutes or until knife inserted in center comes clean. Serve immediately.

broccoli casserole

sweet-and-sour celery

Yield: 6 servings

1 bunch fresh celery
4 slices bacon
1 small onion, sliced into rings
¼ cup white vinegar
1 tablespoon sugar
¼ teaspoon salt
¼ teaspoon white pepper

sweet-and-sour celery

Wash and trim celery; cut stalks into 1-inch diagonal pieces.

Fry bacon in large frypan until crisp. Drain on paper towels. Drain bacon fat except 2 tablespoons.

Add celery and onion to hot bacon fat; sauté 6 to 8 minutes, stirring often. Reduce heat; cover. Cook 10 to 12 minutes or until vegetables are just tender. Stir in vinegar, sugar, salt, and pepper; heat through.

Place mixture in serving dish; crumble bacon over top.

maple-sautéed carrots

Yield: 4 to 5 servings

4 cups carrots, cut into 1½-inch strips, julienne-style (about 1 pound)
¼ cup butter or margarine
½ teaspoon cornstarch
¼ cup pure maple syrup
1 teaspoon dry mustard
¾ teaspoon salt

Sauté carrots in butter 6 to 8 minutes, until tender-crisp.

Blend cornstarch with maple syrup until smooth. Stir syrup, mustard, and salt into carrots. Stir-fry about 5 minutes, until carrots are just tender. (If more cooking is desired, cover and simmer 5 more minutes.)

sesame-sautéed carrots

Yield: 5 to 6 servings

3 tablespoons sesame seeds
2½ tablespoons vegetable oil
4 cups grated carrots
Salt to taste

Sauté sesame seeds in oil until brown. Add carrots; stir-fry quickly 1 to 2 minutes. Salt and serve.

mushrooms baked in cheese sauce

Yield: 4 servings

8 large mushrooms
1 tablespoon vegetable oil

cheese sauce

2 tablespoons butter or margarine
2 tablespoons flour
¼ teaspoon salt
1 cup milk
1 cup freshly grated Parmesan cheese
2 tablespoons finely minced scallions
¾ cup fine bread crumbs

Remove stems from mushrooms. Reserve caps; chop stems. Sauté chopped mushrooms in hot oil until most fat is absorbed. Set aside.

Make sauce. Melt butter in saucepan over low heat. Blend in flour and salt; stir to break up lumps. Add milk; heat, stirring constantly, until mixture is thick and bubbling. Add ¾ cup cheese; stir to melt. Add scallions and chopped mushrooms.

Arrange mushroom caps, round-side-down, in shallow baking dish. Pour Cheese Sauce over; sprinkle crumbs on top. Sprinkle remaining cheese evenly over bread crumbs. Bake in preheated 350°F oven 20 minutes or until topping is browned. (After baking, if darker browning is desired, place under broiler 2 to 3 minutes.)

*mushrooms baked
in cheese sauce*

zucchini and tomato casserole

Yield: 4 servings

    4 tablespoons vegetable oil
    1 small onion, chopped
    ½ clove garlic, minced
    2 zucchini squash, sliced
    2 tomatoes, peeled, or 1 cup canned tomatoes
    ½ teaspoon salt
    ½ teaspoon basil
    ¼ teaspoon black pepper
    2 tablespoons grated Parmesan cheese

Heat oil in heavy frypan; sauté onion and garlic. Stir in zucchini; cover. Cook until vegetables are tender. Add tomatoes, salt, basil, and pepper. Cook, uncovered, until mixture is well-blended, about 10 minutes. Sprinkle with cheese. Place under broiler a few minutes to brown top.

stuffed zucchini and tomatoes

Yield: 8 servings

    4 medium zucchini
    ½ cup water
    2 cups fine bread crumbs
    ⅛ teaspoon oregano
    ⅓ cup butter or margarine, softened
    1 small garlic clove, mashed through press
    ¼ teaspoon salt
    ¼ cup shredded Swiss cheese
    ¼ cup freshly grated Parmesan cheese
    4 firm ripe tomatoes
    ½ teaspoon minced scallions
    2 teaspoons finely chopped fresh parsley
    ½ teaspoon dried tarragon
    3 tablespoons butter or margarine, melted

Trim ends of zucchini; cut in half lengthwise. Place zucchini halves, cut-side-down, in large skillet. Add water; cover. Cook over low heat 10 minutes. Remove; cool. Carefully scoop pulp from centers into bowl. Drain off water from pulp. Mash pulp with fork; add *half* of following combined ingredients: bread crumbs, oregano, softened butter, garlic, salt, and Swiss cheese. Blend thoroughly. Spoon into squash shells; sprinkle tops with half the Parmesan cheese. Place filled squash in large shallow baking pan.

Cut tomatoes in half crosswise; scoop out centers. Drain tomato shells by turning cut-side-down. Combine tomato pulp and stuffing ingredients remaining from above. Spoon into shells; sprinkle tops with remaining Parmesan cheese. Place tomato halves in pan with zucchini. Sprinkle minced scallions, parsley, and tarragon on tops. Drizzle small amount melted butter over each stuffed vegetable. Bake in preheated 375°F oven 15 minutes or until stuffing bubbles. Place under broiler about 3 minutes to brown tops. Serve hot.

zucchini and cheese bake

Yield: 4 servings

2 medium zucchini squash, sliced
1 small onion, chopped
2 tablespoons vegetable oil

½ pound cottage cheese
½ teaspoon basil
2 tablespoons Parmesan cheese

Sauté zucchini and onion in hot oil; drain.
Puree cottage cheese and basil in blender.
Alternate layers of cottage cheese and zucchini in greased ovenproof casserole dish. Sprinkle Parmesan cheese on top. Bake, uncovered, at 350°F 20 to 25 minutes.

stuffed zucchini and tomatoes

salads

starting sprouts

Yield: Approximately 1 quart

materials needed

Seeds for sprouting
1 wide-mouth quart glass jar
Clean cheesecloth or nylon stocking to fit over mouth of jar
Rubber band or screw-top ring to fit jar mouth

Place 2 tablespoons seeds in clean jar. Place cheesecloth over mouth of jar. Stretch tightly; fasten with rubber band or screw-top ring. Fill jar half-full with luke-warm water. Let stand overnight.

Next morning pour out water. Rinse 2 or 3 times with fresh lukewarm water; drain well. Place jar on its side in dark cupboard, shaking gently to distribute seeds along side of jar.

Remove jar from cupboard 2 or 3 times a day; repeat rinsing procedure. (Meal-times are good times to remember to rinse seeds.) Drain well each time; place jar back on its side in dark cupboard.

After rinsing on morning of third or fourth day (depending on type of seed and length of sprouts), drain; place jar on sunny windowsill several hours, until sprouts turn green.

Remove cheesecloth. Fill jar to overflowing with fresh water. Hold sprouts in place with hands while many seed coats wash away; drain well. Store in refrigerator like lettuce. Use within 1 week.

banana waldorf salad

Yield: 4 servings

3 medium red apples, cored,
    cut into ½-inch pieces
1 banana, peeled, diced
1 stalk celery, diced
¼ cup coarsely chopped walnuts

⅓ cup chopped dates or pitted prunes
3 tablespoons mayonnaise
1 teaspoon honey
Dash of lemon juice

Combine all ingredients; toss lightly. Serve in lettuce cups.

feta-cheese salad

Yield: 4 servings

½ pound feta cheese
Freshly ground black pepper (about ½ teaspoon)
2 tablespoons vegetable oil
2 tablespoons white vinegar
3 stalks celery
10 pecans or walnuts
½ teaspoon salt

Cut cheese in thin slices; arrange in shallow bowl. Sprinkle generously with pepper. Drizzle 1 tablespoon each oil and vinegar over cheese.

Clean celery stalks; cut into thin slices. Arrange on cheese. Sprinkle with nuts. Drizzle with remaining oil and vinegar; sprinkle with salt. Cover; refrigerate at least 1 hour. Mix well; correct seasoning if necessary.

feta-cheese salad

fruit salad with nuts

Yield: 4 to 6 servings

1 small honeydew melon
2 oranges
1 cup blue grapes

Lettuce leaves
12 walnut halves

Scoop out melon with melon-baller.
Cut peel from oranges. Remove white membrane; slice crosswise.
Cut grapes in half; remove seeds.
Line glass bowl with lettuce leaves. Arrange melon balls, orange slices, grapes, and walnuts in layers on top of lettuce.

salad dressing

1 8-ounce container yogurt
1 tablespoon lemon juice
1 tablespoon orange juice
1 tablespoon tomato catsup

2 tablespoons evaporated milk
Dash of salt
Dash of white pepper

Mix and blend well all dressing ingredients. Adjust seasonings.
Pour dressing over fruit. Let salad ingredients marinate 30 minutes. Toss salad just before serving.

fruit salad with nuts

marinated cherry-tomato salad

Yield: 2 to 4 servings

> ¼ cup vegetable oil
> 3 tablespoons cider vinegar
> ½ teaspoon tarragon
> ½ teaspoon basil
> 2 tablespoons chopped fresh parsley
> ¼ teaspoon salt
> 1¼ teaspoons sugar
> Freshly ground pepper to taste
> 1 cup cherry tomatoes
> 1 cup sliced mushrooms (¼ pound)

Combine all but tomatoes and mushrooms in small mixing bowl.

Wash tomatoes; remove stems. Cut in halves. Add tomatoes and mushrooms to dressing in bowl.

Stir gently to coat with dressing. Cover; chill 3 to 4 hours, stirring occasionally during marinating period.

To serve, remove tomatoes and mushrooms from dressing; place on bed of lettuce.

Note: If this salad is made in bowl with leakproof cover, bowl can be turned upside down several times while marinating; mushrooms will be bruised less than if stirred.

cheese-stuffed tomatoes

Yield: 4 servings

> 4 medium tomatoes
> 2 ounces blue cheese
> 2 ounces cottage cheese
> 2 tablespoons evaporated milk
> 1 stalk celery
> ¼ teaspoon salt
> ¼ teaspoon paprika
> ½ teaspoon chopped chives
> 4 lettuce leaves

cheese-stuffed tomatoes

Wash tomatoes. Slice off tops; scoop out seeds.

Crumble blue cheese with fork; blend with cottage cheese and milk.

Mince celery; add to cheese. Season with salt and paprika.

Fill tomatoes with cheese mixture. Sprinkle chopped chives over tops. Place tomato tops back on.

Serve tomatoes on lettuce leaves.

breads and granolas

apricot bran loaf

Yield: 9 × 5-inch loaf

1 cup dried fruit (apricots, pears,
   prunes, or apples)
Boiling water
2 tablespoons sugar
1½ cups sifted all-purpose flour
½ cup sugar

4 teaspoons baking powder
½ teaspoon salt
1½ cups whole-bran cereal
1 cup milk
2 eggs, slightly beaten
⅓ cup vegetable oil

Cut dried fruit into small pieces with scissors. Pour boiling water over fruit to cover. Soak 10 minutes; drain well. Stir 2 tablespoons sugar into fruit.

Sift together flour, ½ cup sugar, baking powder, and salt.

Mix together cereal, milk, eggs, and oil. Add cereal–egg mixture to flour mixture; stir until moistened. Stir in fruit. Pour into greased 9 × 5-inch bread pan. Bake in preheated 350°F oven 1 hour. Remove from pan; cool on rack.

bran whole-wheat bread

Yield: Two 9 × 5-inch loaves

1 cup water
¾ cup milk
¾ cup coarse bran
½ cup molasses
1 tablespoon salt

6 tablespoons butter or margarine
½ cup very warm water
2 packages active dry yeast
3 cups whole-wheat flour (unsifted)
3 cups white all-purpose flour (unsifted)

Heat 1 cup water and milk to boiling point. Stir in bran, molasses, salt, and butter. Cook to lukewarm if necessary.

Put warm water and yeast into large warm bowl; stir until dissolved. Add bran mixture and whole-wheat flour; beat until smooth. Add enough white flour to make dough stiff enough to knead. Knead on floured board 8 to 10 minutes or until smooth and elastic. Place in greased bowl; turn once to grease top. Cover; let rise until double (about 45 minutes).

Punch down dough; shape into 2 loaves. Place in 2 greased 9 × 5-inch loaf pans; cover. Let rise until dough reaches tops of pans.

Bake in preheated 375° oven 45 minutes or until done. Remove from pans; cool on racks.

date nut bread

Yield: 1 loaf (9 × 5 inches)

1 cup boiling water
1 8-ounce package pitted dates, chopped
¼ cup shortening
½ cup all-purpose flour
1 cup whole-wheat flour
¼ cup wheat germ
½ cup sugar
1 teaspoon baking soda
¼ teaspoon salt
1 egg, slightly beaten
¾ cup sliced almonds

Pour boiling water over dates. Add shortening; let stand.

Meanwhile combine flours, wheat germ, sugar, soda, and salt. Stir in date mixture, egg, and ½ cup almonds; mix well. Spoon batter into greased loaf pan. Sprinkle reserved nuts on top. Bake at 350°F 50 minutes or until done. Test for doneness with cake-tester or toothpick. Remove from pan; cool on rack.

date nut bread

pumpkin bread

Yield: Two 9 × 5-inch loaves

- ⅔ cup shortening
- 2½ cups sugar
- 4 eggs
- 2 cups cooked pumpkin
- ⅔ cup water
- 1 cup all-purpose flour
- 2 cups whole-wheat flour
- 2 teaspoons baking soda
- 1½ teaspoons salt
- ½ teaspoon baking powder
- 1 teaspoon ground cloves
- 1 teaspoon ground cinnamon
- ⅔ cup chopped nuts
- 1 cup raisins

Cream shortening and sugar in large bowl. Blend in eggs, pumpkin, and water.

Combine remaining ingredients, except nuts and raisins, in separate bowl. Add to pumpkin mixture; mix well. Stir in nuts and raisins. Pour into 2 greased 9 × 5-inch loaf pans. Bake at 350°F 60 to 70 minutes or until done.

rye bread

rye bread

Yield: 2 round loaves

- 2 packages dry yeast
- ½ cup warm water
- 1½ cups lukewarm milk
- 2 tablespoons sugar
- 1 teaspoon salt
- ½ cup molasses
- 2 tablespoons butter or margarine
- 2 tablespoons caraway seeds (optional)
- 3¼ cups unsifted rye flour
- 2½ cups unsifted all-purpose flour

Dissolve yeast in warm water.

Combine milk, sugar, and salt in large bowl. Use mixer to beat in molasses, butter, yeast mixture, caraway seeds if desired, and 1 cup rye flour. Use wooden spoon to mix in remaining rye flour. Add white flour by stirring until dough is stiff enough to knead. Knead 5 to 10 minutes, adding flour as needed. If dough sticks to hands and board, add more flour. Cover dough; let rise 1 to 1½ hours or until double.

Punch down dough; divide to form 2 round loaves. Let loaves rise on greased baking sheet until double, about 1½ hours.

Preheat oven to 375°F. Bake bread 30 to 35 minutes.

granola

Yield: 12 cups

> 6 cups rolled oats
> 2 cups wheat flakes (or rolled oats)
> 1 cup chopped cashew nuts
> 1 cup unsweetened flaked coconut
> 1 cup wheat germ
> ½ cup instant dry milk powder
> 3 tablespoons flax seeds (optional)
> 2 tablespoons brewer's yeast
> ½ cup vegetable oil, preferably safflower
> ½ cup honey
> 1 tablespoon vanilla

Combine rolled oats and wheat flakes in Dutch oven. Heat, uncovered, in 400°F oven about 45 minutes, until browned. Watch carefully; stir often, especially during last half of browning period.

Remove from oven. Stir in nuts, coconut, wheat germ, milk powder, flax seeds, and yeast. Bake 5 minutes. Remove from oven.

Combine oil, honey, and vanilla; pour over granola. Stir well; place in oven 5 minutes. Remove; let cool thoroughly. Store in airtight container.

fruited almond granola

Yield: 11 cups

> 5 cups rolled oats
> ¾ cup orange juice
> ½ cup wheat germ
> 2 tablespoons nonfat dry milk powder
> ¼ teaspoon salt
> 3 tablespoons vegetable oil
> 3 tablespoons honey
> ¼ teaspoon almond extract
> 1 cup chopped dates
> ½ cup diced dried apricots
> ½ cup diced pitted prunes
> ¾ cup coarsely chopped almonds
> 1½ cups grapenuts cereal

In Dutch oven or large ovenproof casserole dish stir together oats and orange juice until evenly mixed. Bake in 350°F oven until oats are dry and browned, about 40 to 50 minutes. Stir often, especially during last half of browning time.

Combine wheat germ, milk powder, and salt. Stir into oats.

In small pan or metal measuring cup, heat together oil and honey until warm. Add almond extract. Pour over oat mixture; stir until well combined. Place oat mixture back in oven; toast 5 to 7 minutes, stirring if necessary. Stir in remaining ingredients. Cool thoroughly, then store in airtight container.

desserts

apple–grape salad

Yield: 4 servings

> **2 medium tart apples, peeled, quartered, cored**
> **½ pound blue grapes, halved, seeded**
> **1 stalk garden mint (leaves only)**
> **2 teaspoons sugar**
> **2 tablespoons lemon juice**
> **2 tablespoons brandy**

Cut apples crosswise in thin slices. Arrange grapes, apples, and mint leaves in glass bowl. Sprinkle with sugar, lemon juice, and brandy. Toss lightly; cover. Chill 1 hour.

apple–grape salad

baked apples with cranberry filling

baked apples with cranberry filling

Yield: 4 servings

> 4 large apples, cores removed to ½ inch of bottoms
> 8 tablespoons whole cranberry sauce
> 1 tablespoon butter or margarine
> ¾ cup boiling water
> 2 tablespoons sugar

Fill centers of apples with cranberry sauce. Dot tops with butter. Place in 8 × 8-inch pan with ¾ cup boiling water. Bake in preheated 375°F oven 40 to 60 minutes or until tender but not mushy.

Serve apples hot or cold. Sprinkle with sugar just before serving.

cranberry applesauce

Yield: 2½ to 3 quarts

> 5 pounds red apples (about 25 apples)
> ¾ cup water
> 1 pound cranberries
> 1¼ cups sugar, more or less, depending on sweetness of apples

Wash apples; cut into quarters. (Do not peel or core.) Place water and quartered apples in large Dutch oven (5- or 6-quart size).

Wash cranberries; place on top of apples. Cover; bring to boil over medium heat. Lower heat; cook until apples lose their shape and are tender, about ½ hour. Stir occasionally to prevent sticking and to allow apples to cook uniformly. When apples and cranberries are cooked, remove from heat; press through food mill. Sweeten with sugar to taste.

Serve applesauce warm or chilled. Extra applesauce can be frozen or canned.

fruit with honey sauce

Yield: 4 servings

2 peaches, peeled, cubed
2 cups fresh or canned pineapple chunks
2 apples, peeled, cored, cut into rings
1 cup water or pineapple juice
⅓ cup honey
1 thin lemon slice
1 stick cinnamon
1 banana, sliced lengthwise and in half
2 tablespoons sliced almonds
Whipped cream for garnish
4 cherries or grapes

Combine all ingredients, except last 4, in small casserole. Cover; cook at 350°F 40 minutes. Add banana; just heat through.

Serve fruit warm. Garnish each serving with almonds, whipped cream, and a cherry or grape.

fruit with honey sauce

carrot cake

Yield: 10-inch bundt cake

3 eggs, separated
½ cup brown sugar
½ cup sugar
½ cup vegetable oil
2½ teaspoons vanilla
1½ cups whole-wheat pastry flour
1 cup all-purpose flour
2 teaspoons baking soda

½ teaspoon baking powder
½ teaspoon salt
1½ teaspoons cinnamon
¼ teaspoon clove
½ cup milk
2½ cups grated carrots
½ cup grated coconut
½ cup chopped nuts

Beat together egg yolks and sugars. Blend in oil and vanilla. Set aside.

Stir together flours, soda, baking powder, salt, cinnamon, and clove. Add flour mixture to sugar mixture alternately with milk; stir well. Blend in carrots, coconut, and nuts.

Beat egg whites until stiff but not dry. Fold into cake batter just until evenly distributed. Pour into well-greased 10-inch bundt pan. Bake at 350°F 40 to 45 minutes or until cake tests done. Let cool 10 minutes. Remove from pan to rack to finish cooling.

Just before serving, sprinkle with powdered sugar if desired.

chocolate oatmeal cake

Yield: 8-inch-square cake

⅔ cup boiling water
½ cup rolled oats
¼ cup butter or margarine
½ cup packed brown sugar
⅓ cup sugar
¾ teaspoon vanilla
1 egg, beaten
¾ cup whole-wheat pastry flour
½ teaspoon baking powder
½ teaspoon baking soda
¼ teaspoon salt
2 tablespoons cocoa

Pour boiling water over oats. Let stand 15 to 20 minutes.

Cream together butter and sugars. Beat in vanilla and egg. Add oatmeal; beat well.

Stir together flour, baking powder, soda, salt, and cocoa. Add to oatmeal mixture; stir until well blended. Pour into greased 8-inch-square baking pan. Bake at 350°F 25 to 30 minutes or until done.

Serve cake plain, with whipped cream, or sprinkled with confectioners' sugar.

granola doughnuts

Yield: 24 to 30 bite-size doughnuts

1 cup all-purpose flour
½ cup whole-wheat flour
¾ cup sugar
1 teaspoon salt
1½ teaspoons baking powder
1 teaspoon nutmeg
1 egg, beaten

½ cup milk
¼ cup vegetable oil
½ cup Granola (see Index)
½ cup raisins
Oil for frying (oil should be at least 2 inches deep in fryer or saucepan)
1 teaspoon cinnamon

Sift together flours, ¼ cup sugar, salt, baking powder, and nutmeg. Add egg, milk, and ¼ cup oil; beat until smooth. Stir in Granola and raisins.

Heat frying oil to 375°F. Drop batter by teaspoonfuls into hot oil. Cook only about 6 doughnuts at a time to prevent oil from cooling down. Fry doughnuts 1½ to 2 minutes or until light brown. Turn doughnuts when bottoms are brown. Drain on paper towels.

Place ½ cup sugar and cinnamon in paper bag; shake to combine. Place drained doughnuts in bag; shake to coat doughnuts on all sides. Remove doughnuts from bag; cool on racks.

granola doughnuts

baked caramel custard

Yield: 4 servings

> 1 cup sugar
> ¼ cup water
> 1 4- to 6-cup metal mold
> 4 eggs
> 2 egg yolks
> 2½ cups hot milk
> Dash of salt
> 1 teaspoon vanilla

Put ½ cup sugar and water into mold. Heat until sugar caramelizes and turns dark brown. Immediately dip mold into pan of cold water 2 to 3 seconds to cool. Tilt pan so mixture films bottom and sides of mold with caramel.

Combine eggs, yolks, and ½ cup sugar in medium-size bowl; beat until well-mixed and foamy. Stir in 1¼ cups hot milk; mix well. Add remaining milk, salt, and vanilla; stir well. Strain sauce through sieve to remove coagulated egg. Pour into mold. Skim off foam on top.

Preheat oven to 325°F.

Set mold in larger pan. Pour boiling water around mold to come halfway up its sides. Place on lowest oven rack. Bake custard 45 minutes or until center is firm. Cool, then refrigerate custard.

When ready to unmold, run knife around edge; set in lukewarm water 1 or 2 minutes. Place serving plate upside down over mold; quickly invert.

vermont maple–apple pudding

Yield: 4 to 6 servings

> 6 tablespoons butter or margarine
> ¼ cup packed brown sugar
> 1 cup whole-wheat pastry flour
> 2½ teaspoons baking powder
> ¼ teaspoon salt
> ½ teaspoon cinnamon
> 1 cup milk
> ½ cup pure maple syrup
> ½ teaspoon vanilla
> 3 medium apples, peeled, coarsely chopped (2 cups)

Melt butter in 2-quart casserole dish.

Stir together brown sugar, flour, baking powder, salt, and cinnamon.

Combine milk, maple syrup, and vanilla. Pour over flour mixture; blend until smooth. Pour batter over melted butter in casserole; do not stir. Place apples on top of batter. Bake in 375°F oven 35 to 40 minutes, until crust turns brown.

Serve pudding warm with plain cream.

tapioca stewed fruit

Try baking this fragrant dessert on a cold winter day with an "all-oven" meal.

Yield: 6 to 8 servings

¼ cup pearl tapioca
⅔ cup water
1 8-ounce package mixed dried fruit or 8 ounces dried peaches, apricots, and
    pears, mixed
½ cup dried apples, coarsely chopped
½ cup pitted prunes, coarsely chopped
¼ cup currants
¼ cup chopped cranberries
2 cups water
2 cups apricot nectar
½ cup packed brown sugar
½ orange, sliced thinly, seeds removed
½ lemon, sliced thinly, seeds removed
1 cinnamon stick

Soak pearl tapioca in water overnight.
Add remaining ingredients. Pour into 3-quart casserole or Dutch oven; cover.
Bake at 350°F 65 to 75 minutes, until thickened and fruit is soft. Remove from oven;
let set until cool enough to eat. Remove cinnamon stick.
Serve warm, or refrigerate and serve cold.

golden pearl tapioca

Yield: 4 to 5 servings

½ cup pearl tapioca
Water to cover
2 cups warm water
¾ cup nonfat dry milk powder
1 stick cinnamon

⅓ cup packed brown sugar
2 eggs, beaten
½ teaspoon salt
1 teaspoon vanilla

Soak tapioca overnight in water to cover.
Drain tapioca. Place in top of double boiler. Add warm water, dry milk, and
cinnamon stick. Cook over low heat, stirring occasionally, about 50 minutes or until
tapioca is clear.
Beat together sugar, eggs, and salt.
When tapioca has finished cooking, remove cinnamon stick. Add small amount
hot tapioca to egg mixture, then gradually stir egg mixture into tapioca. Cook, stirring, about 5 minutes, but *do not let boil.* Remove from heat. Add vanilla.
Spoon tapioca into dishes. Serve warm or chilled. Cooled mixture will be
thicker.

index